Classic
DROODLES

by ROGER PRICE

PRICE STERN SLOAN

Los Angeles

Copyright 1992, 1974, 1964, 1955, 1954, 1953 by Roger Price
Published by Price Stern Sloan, Inc.
11150 Olympic Boulevard, Sixth Floor
Los Angeles, California 90064
Printed in U.S.A.

10 9 8 7 6 5 4 3 2 1

Library of Congress Catalog Card Number: 91-060216

This book has been printed on acid-free paper.

A Few Words for Posterity ... or Whoever

Droodles are really self-explanatory, but if you are maladjusted and have a block against this peculiar and tenacious sub-artform, you can always ask someone else to explain them (if you don't mind coarse language). Droodles have been called many things (i.e. "Scrabble for Illiterates," "Solitaire for Morons") but they actually are "The Best of All Possible Ways to Waste Time."

They are also a great moral force, because you cannot get into trouble with the law or with the opposite sex if you spend all your time Droodling (neither Richard Nixon nor Spiro Whatshisname were Droodlers). Droodles are also very safe. Safer, for instance, than a battleship. If you consult your almanac you'll find that no Droodle was ever sunk by a dive bomber or a submarine. To carry the comparison further, no Droodle ever made anyone seasick either. Slightly nauseated, perhaps, but never seasick.

One Hundred and Seventy-One Words of Explanation

A Droodle is a borkley-looking sort of drawing that doesn't make any sense until you know the correct title. For instance, here are some classic Droodles that illustrate this point:

This, of course, appears to be "A Mother Pyramid Feeding Its Child," but it isn't. It is called:

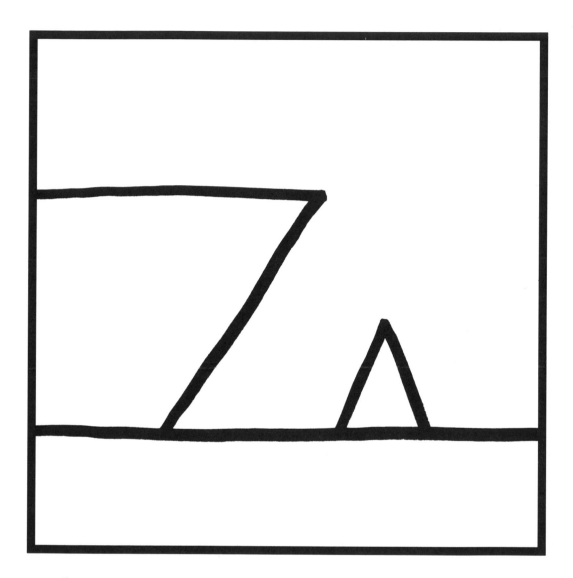

A Ship Arriving Too Late to Save a Drowning Witch

You may think this one is Two Palm Trees on a Desert Island or A Gopher with Two TV Sets. Both wrong. It is:

An Early Bird Who Caught a Very Strong Worm

Now do you understand why Droodles are the greatest invention since coloring for margarine? Do you feel that you could become a Droodler? If not here's an extra classic Droodle. Study it. Can you figure out what it is?

The Outside World as Seen by a Little Man Living in a Beer Can

You now know as much about Droodles as I do (which is plenty), and after studying this book full of splendid examples, you'll be entitled to make up your own. Remember, Droodling requires no talent, no ability—just nerve. Onward.

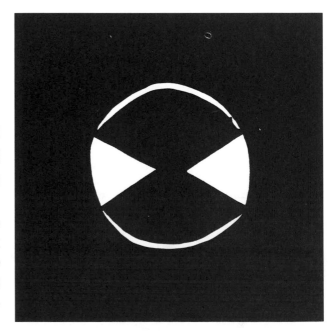

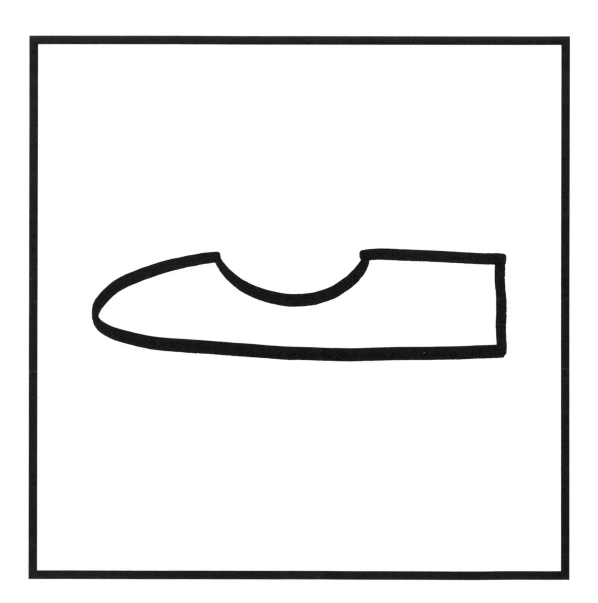

Maternity Ironing Board

Elephant Giving an Ant a Friendly Pat on the Back

Checkerboard for a Hermit

This Droodle was suggested to me by my friend, Leonard Stern. He didn't want me to mention his name but I asked 20 other people and they all refused flatly to take credit for it. One of them even challenged me to a fistfight but he changed his mind when I reported him to his scout master. I don't think it's fair. There's no reason I should take the blame for Droodles I don't think up. I have enough trouble already with libel suits, eviction suits and a crummy herring-bone suit that won't hold a crease. From now on I'm going to give credit where credit is due regardless of the outcome. Just so long as the outcome doesn't affect my income.

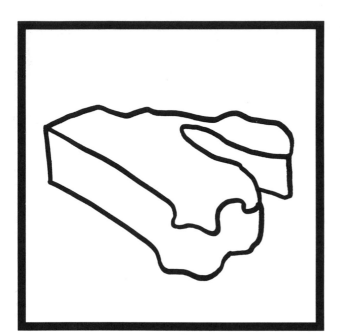

Slip Cover for Rhode Island

Highway for Grasshoppers

**Clock for Telling
What Time It Was**

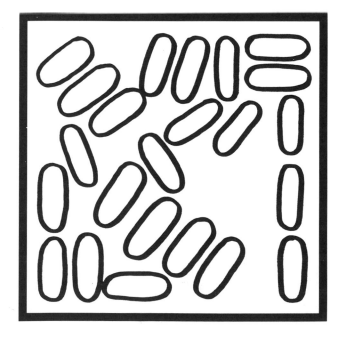

**Aerial View of
Used Bathtub Lot**

11

This Droodle has several (nine to be exact) titles. You may check off whichever you think most appropriate or if you're a troublemaker and don't like any of them you can make up your own.

Doorknob in a Hair Tonic Factory

A Noiseless Ping-Pong Ball

Total Eclipse of a Pin Cushion

Sexy Bagel Wearing False Eyelashes

An Outspoken Wheel

Combination Toothbrush and Doughnut for People Who Don't Have Time to Eat Between Brushings

A Fried Egg That Was Almost Crosshatched

Circular Centipede Under a Beach Umbrella

A Snowball with a Fur Coat

_____

(your title)

Pig Emerging from a Fog Bank

Integrated Club

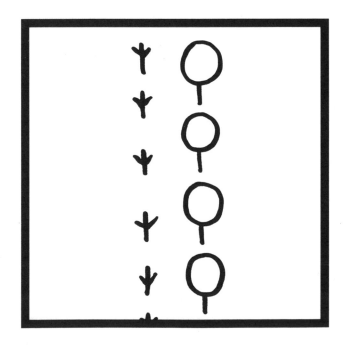

**Tracks Made by a Chicken
Wearing One Snowshoe**

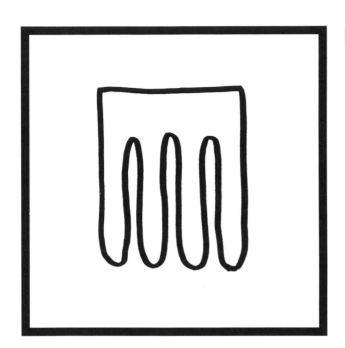

Falsies for a Cow

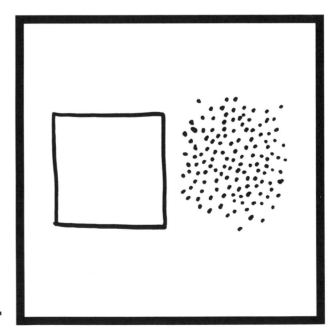

Unassembled Sandpaper

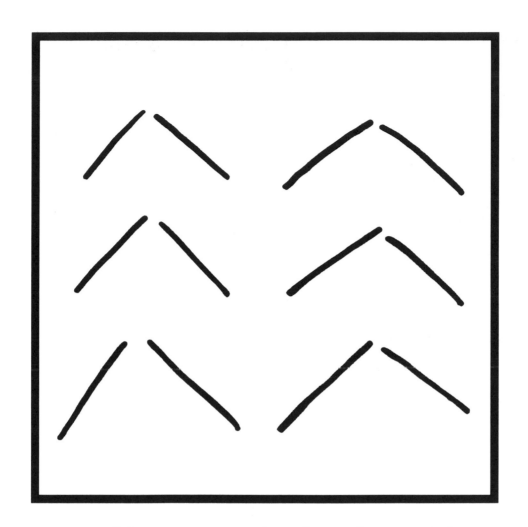

Box of Spare Mustaches for Prince Rainier

or:

A Memorandum from a Parakeet

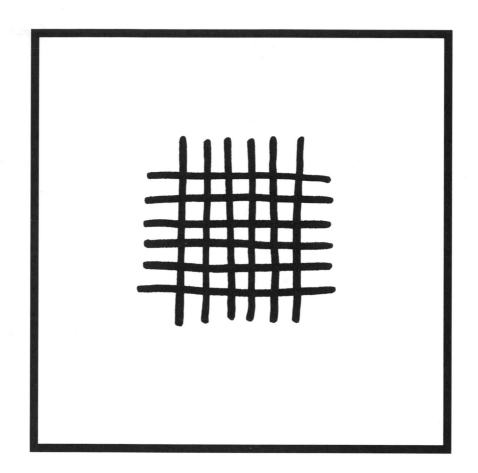

Tic-Tac-Tic-Tac-Tic-Tac-Toe Game

or:

A Waffle with the Mange

or:

Sauerkraut Served by Neat Waiter

Two Ants Trying to Join a Golf Club

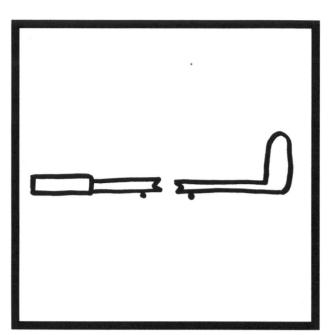

Centipede Proposing

A Porcupump

I discovered this Droodle one day in a subway station in New York. It was scratched on the wall along with a lot of other important information. Stuff like: "Fats loves Madelyn" and "Joe's sister puts spaghetti in her shoes" and "Jean Paul Sartre is a fink." There was also a phone number with this message scratched beside it: "I'm a lovely, lonesome 18-year-old girl with lots of money. Please call." But I'm not fool enough to pay attention to junk like that. Besides it was a wrong number.

Coat Hanger for a Nudist

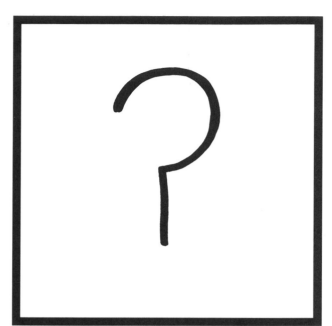

**Recording of the
Unfinished Symphony**

21

Toothbrush for Honeymooners

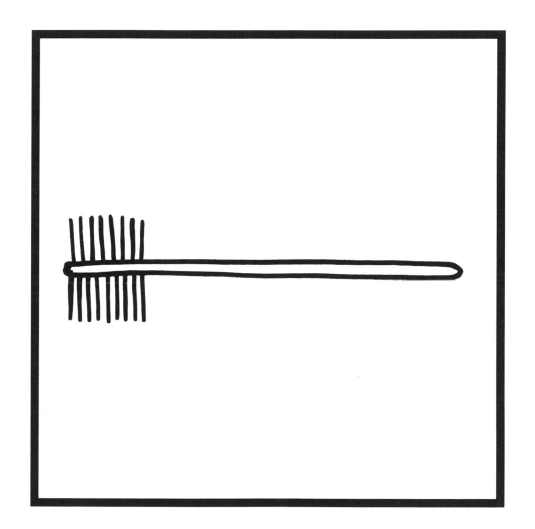

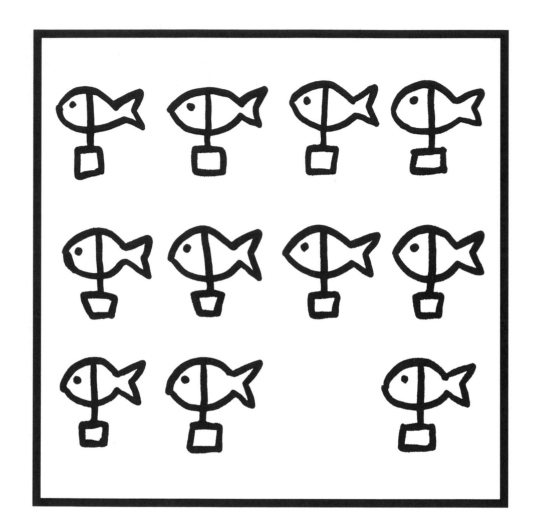

School of Fish with Dropout

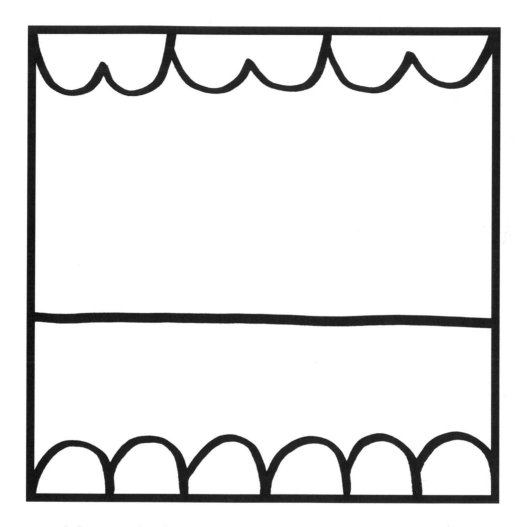

Bald-Headed Men Watching Burlesque Show

Glasses for Woman Who Had Her Face Lifted

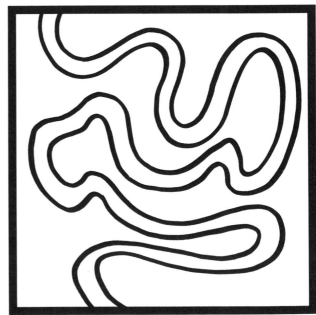

Highway Designed by Politician Whose Brother Owns Cement Company

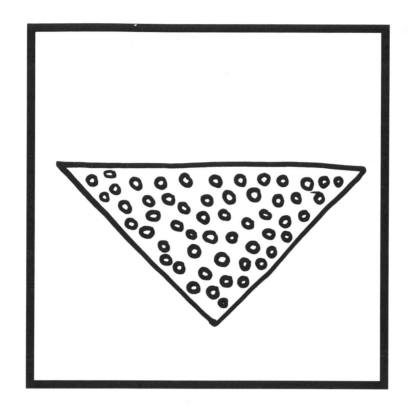

Diaper for Baby Porcupine

Dr. Schwine says the correct title for this Droodle should be: "An Air-Conditioned Pyramid." In fact, he claims he saw such a pyramid eight years ago in South America when the Schwine-Kitzenger Expedition was trying to locate the lost city of Xotptyl in Peru. The expedition started when Dr. Schwine copied a secret map from the screen while watching a Tony Curtis movie but they eventually had to give up. After five months, not only had they been unable to find the Hidden City, they hadn't even found Peru. However, the trip wasn't a total loss. They were able to sell the poison darts they picked out of Mrs. Schwine to a museum for over $400.

Screen Star

Father Cannonball Out Walking Little BBs

or if you turn the page sideways:

A Bowling Ball with a Leak

Inside View of Napoleon's Coat

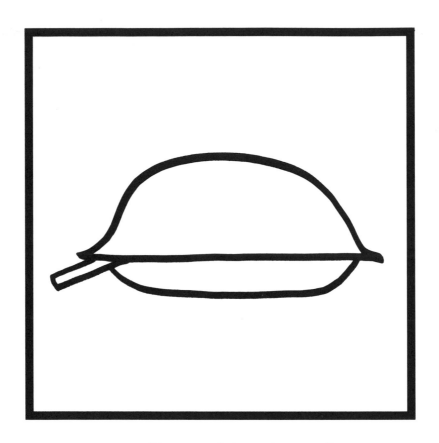

Turtle Smoking in Bed

Some people may say this isn't a Droodle children should see because it will give them ideas. Well, I discussed it in advance with a psychologist and he told me the only idea it will give children is that they can draw funnier Droodles than I can. This psychologist is a troublemaker.

An Egyptian Bowling Ball

Kit for Building a Square Dog*

This Droodle was given to me by Larry Sloan who suggested I show it to Dr. Schwine. Dr. Schwine looked at it and said, "Not bad, but it isn't as clever as my 'Geiger Subtractor for People Who Want to Lose Uranium.' If this fellow wants to call himself an inventor he'll have to come up with something that's really practical like my 'Combination Tombstone and Picnic Table.' Or my patented 'False Teeth with Cavities for People Who Still Want to See Their Dentist Twice a Year.' "

I hope this constructive criticism doesn't discourage Larry, but it probably will.

*a box terrier

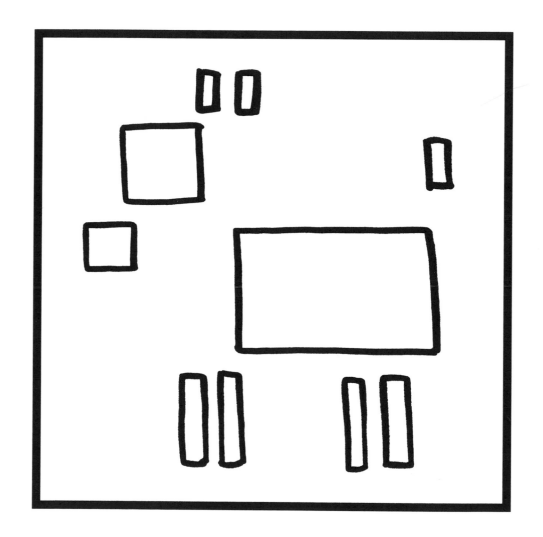

You have to use a lot of imagination to understand these titles. They are so looney they even worry me.

A Dishonest Butterfly Tilting a Pinball Machine

Ranch-Type Phone Booth with a P.A. System

A Modernistic Lump

A Robot Blowing a Bugle in a Bathtub

An Up-Wrong Piano

A Nincom with a Pooped Poop

_____

(I give up. You try.)

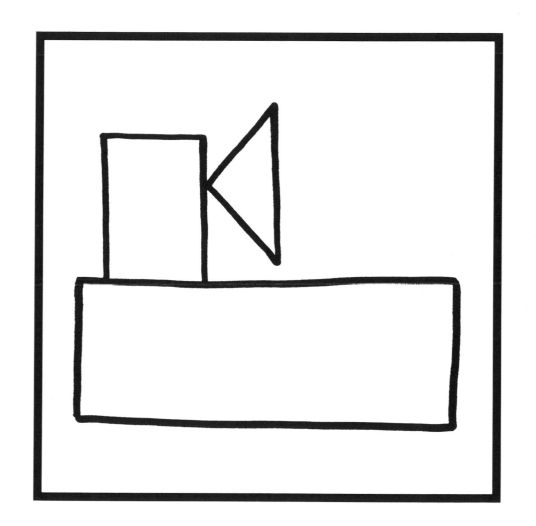

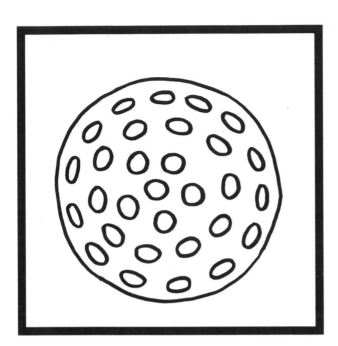

A Bowling Ball for a Man Who Likes to Make Decisions

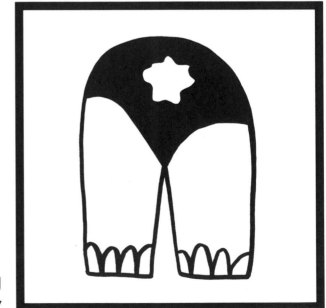

Elephant Auditioning for Job as Playboy Bunny

Eggs with Windows for People Who Like to Count Their Chickens Before They're Hatched

Fish Committing Suicide

This fish isn't really committing suicide. It's a publicity shot of a starlet in a new underwater television series "Subnanza" which eliminates people altogether. It stars Flipper and Sandra Crab in an honest, fishy heartwarming tale. Flipper, who is really in love with Sandra, has to get engaged to an ugly lady octopus who holds the mortgage on her shell. Naturally Miss Crab is heartbroken until her father (played by Roddy McLobster) saves the day by proving that the Octopus already has a husband (played by Squid Caesar). The finale is a hilarious scene in a Prawn Shop with Octopus trying to hock her eight engagement rings. A great program but don't tune it in unless you're sure your set doesn't leak.

A Rolling Stone That Gathered Moss and Also Three Tickets for Speeding

A Three-Carat Ring with Strings Attached

A Footprint Made by a Wounded Bork

_____

(your title)

Box of Spare Parts for a Porcupine

or:

Toupee for Mechanical Man

Space Capsule for a Giraffe

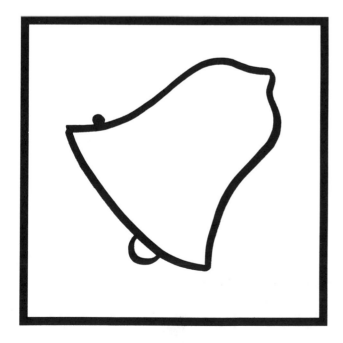

Bug About to Be Tolled Off

This one has the most titles yet. All of them are correct.

Flying Saucer Traffic Jam

Close-Up of the Flag Used at Custer's Last Stand

Script for a Spot Announcement

Bunch of Bleached Eightballs

Burgled Bagels (with Their Holes Stole)

Tracks Left by Pogo Stick Parade

Very Close-Up of Freckle Champ

Gopher Housing Development

Outside World as Seen by a Man Living in a Salt Shaker

Spots for an Albino Leopard

Box of Chicken Pox

52-Ring Flea Circus

Do-It-Yourself Swiss Cheese Kit

Explosion in a Pizza Factory

Man Playing Trombone in Phone Booth

If you identified this one, it shows you are artistic.

The alternate title to this Droodle is found by turning the drawing upside down. It then becomes:

Midget Playing Trombone in Phone Booth

If you turn the picture on its side, counterclockwise, it is subject to a third interpretation:

Deceased Trombone Player

Not only is this an extremely clever Droodle but it affords you a certain amount of exercise which you probably need.

Man in Refrigerator Signaling for Left Turn

The man in this refrigerator is my Uncle Frank who became an ice cream addict a few years back. When his friends would head for the local saloon Uncle Frank would sneak into Doc Skeens' drugstore and spend the evening lapping up sodas and sundaes. At about 11 o'clock he'd start to get rowdy and put the comic books back in the wrong racks and make paper chains out of the soda straws and Doc would give him a pint of vanilla crunch for a nightcap and send him home. Before breakfast he always had three or four dixie cups which he called "eye-openers" and for lunch he'd have a quart of tutti-frutti on the rocks. Well Aunt Margaret finally called the State Hospital for help, and when the man in the white coat came, Uncle Frank welcomed him with open arms. He thought he was a Good Humor® man.

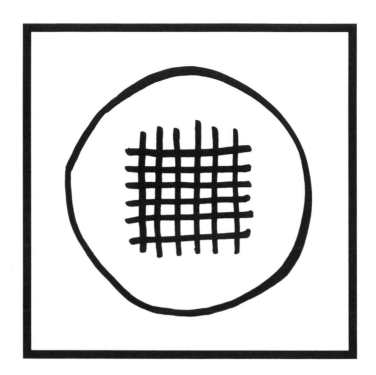

Mended Doughnut

By this time you can see that Droodling is as easy as falling off a log. In fact, we've found that people who have fallen off logs make the best Droodlers.

If you aren't interested in doughnuts or dunking, here is an alternate title for the Droodle:

Six Cents' Worth of Screen Wire

If you don't like the alternate title, here is another:

Plate of Spaghetti Served by Neat Waiter

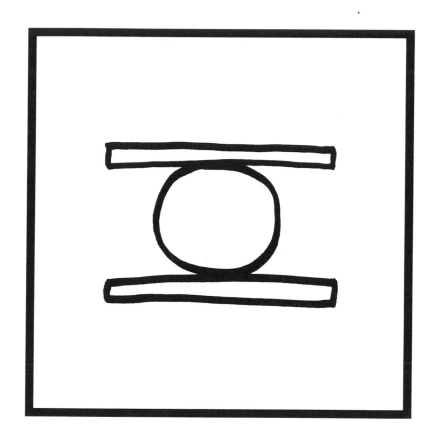

Tomato Sandwich Made by
Amateur Tomato Sandwich Maker

A number of former friends to whom I showed this Droodle said it was a typical example of something that would only appeal to a ten-year-old mentality. These people are typical examples of the Wrong Thinkers who are jealous of me. I showed this Droodle to a ten-year-old and it didn't appeal to him. He said he thought it was "coo-koo." I had to go to a child of six before I got any real appreciation.

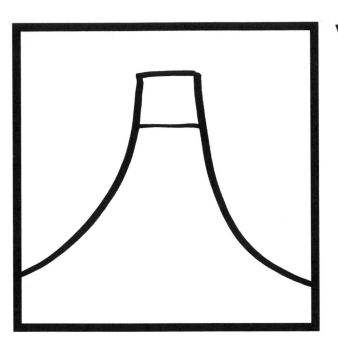

Volcano with Filter Tip

**Tower of Pisa
as Seen by Leaning Tourist**

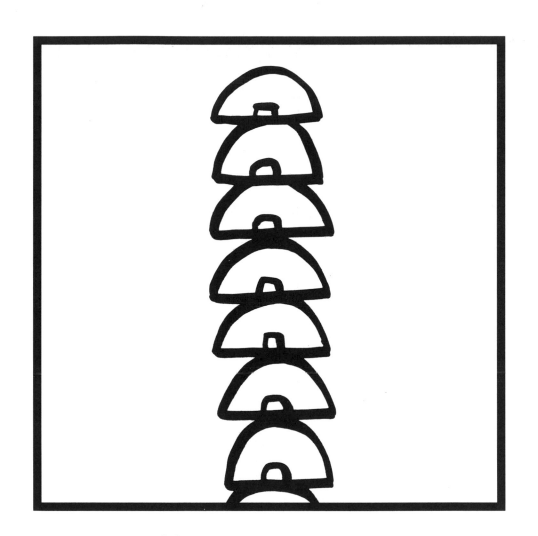

Eskimo Apartment House

Worm Taking Date to Dinner

I thought up this Droodle while doing push-ups to keep my weight down. Everyone should exercise and try to keep their weight down. My colleague, Dr. Schwine, recently stated it rather well when he said, "Too many loaves in the bread basket mean trouble." He based this pithy comment on a study the Schwine-Kitzenger Institute just made of 47 men who were over 100 years old. They found that these men over 100 years old all had several things in common:

(1) They all had moderate appetites.

(2) They all came from middle-class homes.

(3) All but two of them were dead.

Clam with Buck Teeth

This Droodle might also be entitled:

A Football with a Picture Window

but it shouldn't be. Because it portrays one of the pedigreed clams which I breed to enter in the big Bivalve Show at Madison Square Garden every year. This particular clam (registered as "Prince Kenmore of Oden," call name "Buck") never won any blue ribbons but he had such an infectious personality I used to keep him in the house on the coffee table. But he was also very curious and every time I had a party he'd open his shell to see what was going on and always ended up with a face full of cigarette butts. So I moved him to a safer place, back on the patio next to my Spanish shawl, and he eventually came to a bad end. He fell in love with a castanet and had a nervous breakdown trying to click his shell back at it in rumba tempo.

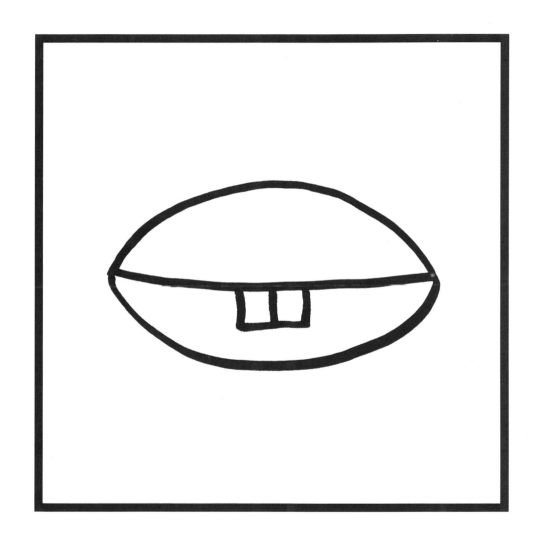

English Sheep Girl

The model for this Droodle wasn't an English girl but a friend of mine named Chickie Cossayuna who plays guitar and sings with a folk-rock group called "The Cockroaches." Chickie refers to the Beatles as having crew cuts and claims he likes wearing his hair like this. When he's riding a bus he never feels bad when an old lady has to stand up because he can't see her. And he never has to brush his teeth because when he eats his bangs act as dental floss. Of course there are drawbacks to this haircut. When he gets dressed he often puts his shirt on backwards and when he watches television, all the programs (and everything else) look like the side of a horse. But by and large Chickie is a happy fellow whose motto is, "Keep smiling." I often wonder if he does.

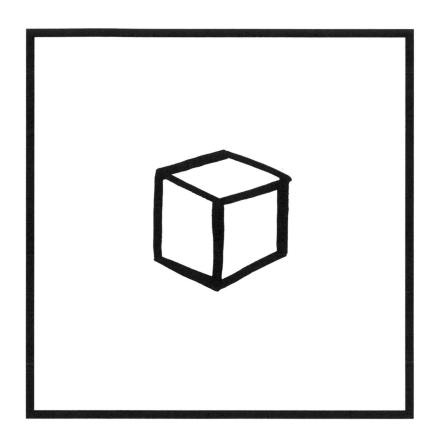

Tennis Ball (Factory Reject)

If you identified this Droodle as a

Volley Ball (Factory Reject)

it shows you are overweight. If you called it merely

A Cube

it shows that you are a square.

Famous Scientist Seen Through Microscope

Actually this is not just any scientist, as the careless looker might think. It happens to be an historic view of Louis Pasteur on the occasion of people first being discovered by germs.

Up until this time germs had thought of people as being either "breakfast," "lunch" or "dinner." But from this point on, in spite of the fact that people are so large they can only be seen when reduced 10,000 or more diameters by expensive optical instruments, it has been held that people have consciousness and experience a complicated emotional and intellectual life.

This advanced view is not held by all germs. There are certain groups of spirochetes who still maintain that people are merely unfeeling lumps of Spam-like substance produced by erosion and spontaneous combustion during the Dark Ages (1902-1928).

This latter explanation, I might add, is highly improbable.*

*For one thing, it doesn't explain how they can be so noisy. Or have traffic accidents. Insensible lumps do not have traffic–much less traffic accidents. These show social organization, intelligence and bad judgment regarding distances, all of which could only evolve in a civilized economy.

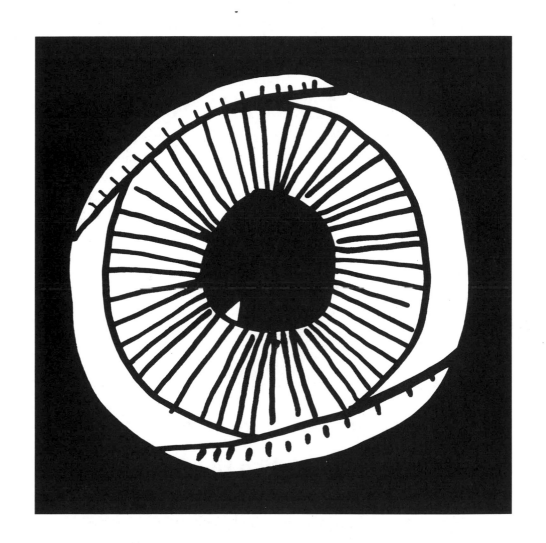

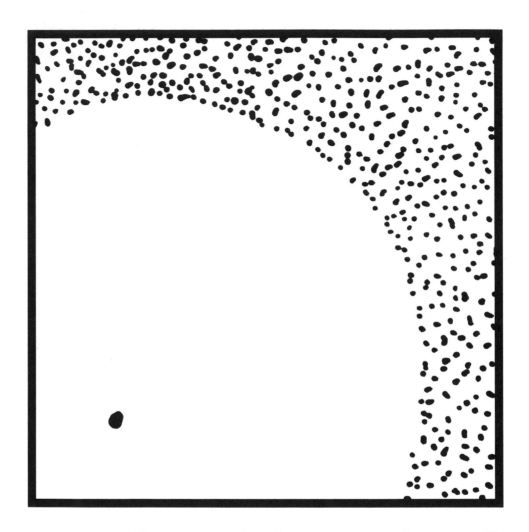

Germs Avoiding Friend Who Has Caught Penicillin

Determined Worm Crawling Over Razor Blade

These Droodles are what we here at headquarters call "Classic Types." This means they're artistically satisfying, have composition and balance, and are so simple any four-year-old can draw them—those over four may have a little trouble.

Man in Tuxedo Who Stood Too Close to the Front of an Elevator

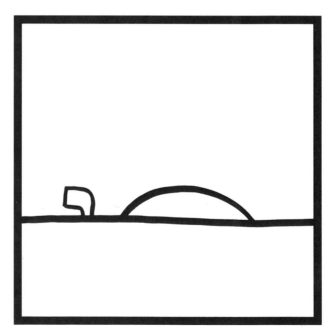

Fat Man Smoking Pipe in Soft Bed

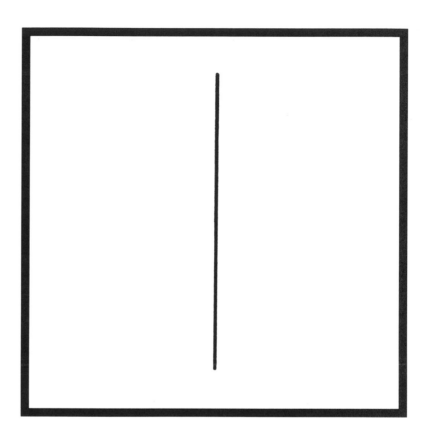

Used All Day Sucker

If this is confusing don't worry as there is another perfectly valid answer. If you turn the page sideways, it becomes:

Postcard, Side View

Four Elephants
Inspecting a Grapefruit

Incidentally, when I was helping to write *The Elephant Book* I learned much more than necessary about these fun-loving creatures. For instance: elephants are not found in America. They aren't found because no one ever loses an elephant in America. But if you would like to find an elephant (it'll give you something to do if your television set and Scrabble® board are both busted) here's what you do. First, get an elephant and lose it. Then search the house thoroughly to make sure the elephant isn't playing "No Peeky" with you by hiding behind a sofa or in a closet. Then go outside and ask everyone if they've noticed an elephant. If this fails, put an ad in the newspaper. But be sure to include an accurate description otherwise you're liable to get someone else's elephant, or a hippopotamus, or a cement mixer.

Another interpretation might be;

Four Unsportsmanlike Gopher Hunters

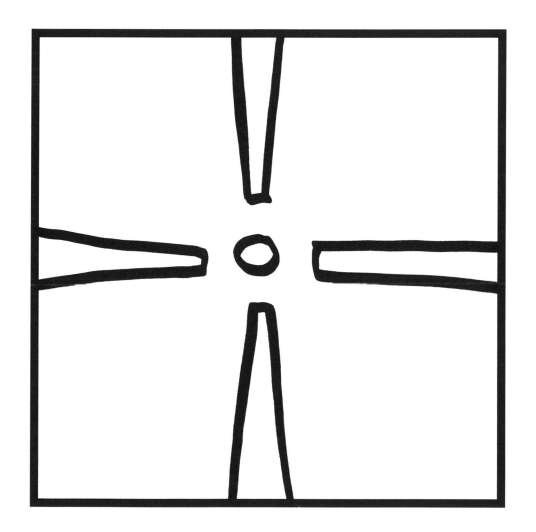

GI
CCCCCCCC

G.I. Over Seas

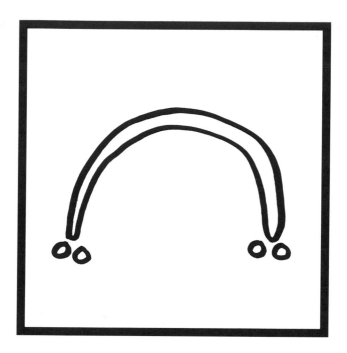

Next time you're feeling neglected at a party (or anywhere) draw this graphic design on something and show it around. Keep showing it around until someone says, "What is that supposed to be?" You explain that it is a dandy picture of

A Worm Rollerskating

If you still feel neglected, assume a confident manner and say that it could also be titled

A Greedy Rainbow with Four Pots

or possibly,

The Entrance to the Holland Tunnel on Wheels

Three Degrees Below Zero

I personally like these Droodles because they give me a chance to show off my printing ability. I learned to print early in life because my handwriting looked exactly like chicken tracks. In fact, once when I wrote something for a handwriting expert who analyzed character, she told me, "You are vain, self-possessed, like corn and lay four eggs a week." But my handwriting got so bad even I couldn't tell what I was writing (and who knows it might have been interesting), so I went to night school and took a course in non-objective penmanship and today my handwriting is entirely different. Now it looks like mongoose tracks.

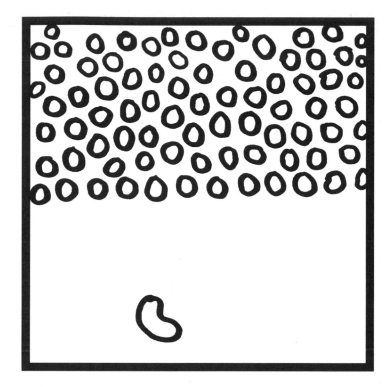

Patriotic Bean Trying to Join Peas Corps

I've made up a story about this Droodle which should give you a deeper insight into the problems of vegetables. The story opens with two French Peas, Pierre Pea and Yvonne Pea (upper left corner), who are happily married and making plans to have some little sprouts. Then along comes the Lima Bean, a political refugee from a pot of Russian cabbage soup who managed to defect by riding piggyback on a Mexican jumping bean. The two peas befriend him, but right away he begins flirting with Yvonne, and now he's demanding to be made an equal pod-ner in their business which is growing. I predict this no-good Lima will come to a bad end—like this story.

Eiffel Tower as Seen by Guard in Armored Truck

If you turn this drawing upside down we have another Droodle entitled:

Eiffel Tower As Seen by Guard in Armored Truck Which Has Just Been Overturned by a Gang of Apaches

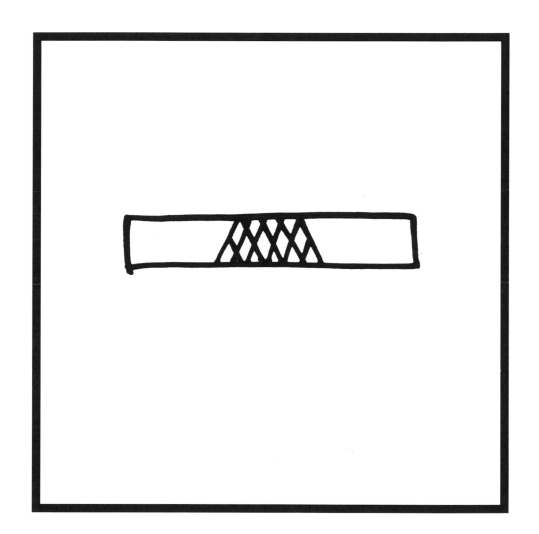

Spider Doing a Handstand

This is an excellent Droodle for the beginner as it can be executed anywhere. If you're in a restaurant, dip your bread in the catsup and go to work on the wall; if driving a friend's convertible, get some grease on your finger and Droodle on the canvas top; if visiting a lady friend, get some of her lipstick over her things for a change. It's also a good starter Droodle because it has so many alternate titles:

Total Eclipse of the Sun on a Stick

A Peace Pipe That Can Be Smoked by Seven Indian Braves and the Chief at the Same Time

Family of Worms Stuck in a Caramel Apple

Frightened Mop

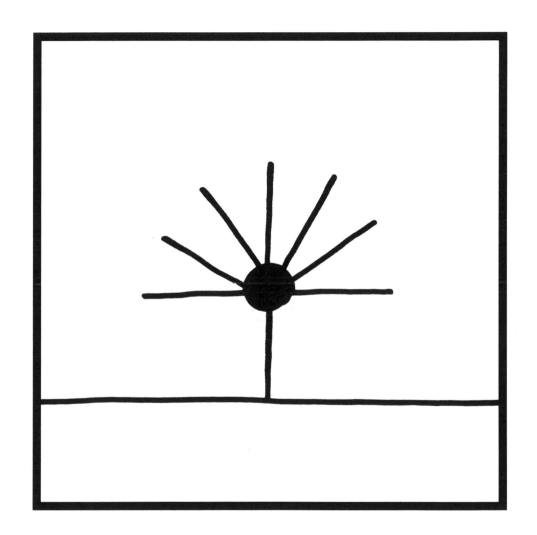

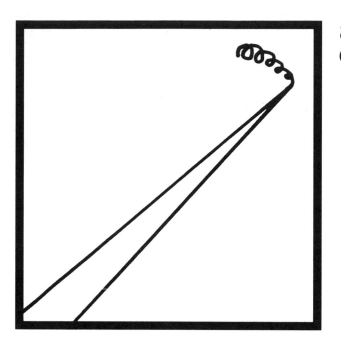

8:12 Train as Seen by 8:12 1/2 Commuter

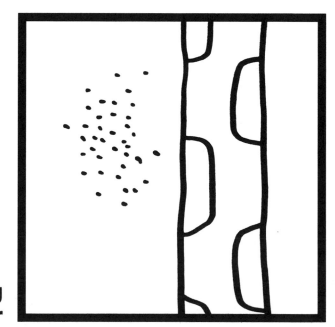

Superstitious Giraffe Throwing Salt Over Left Shoulder

Here is another you can make up your own title for:

**Lima Bean Kicking Away Three Kernels of Corn
Who Have Proposed Succotash**

Baked Potato Blowing Off Steam

A Nurndy Giving Birth to Three Little Nurns

_____

(your title)

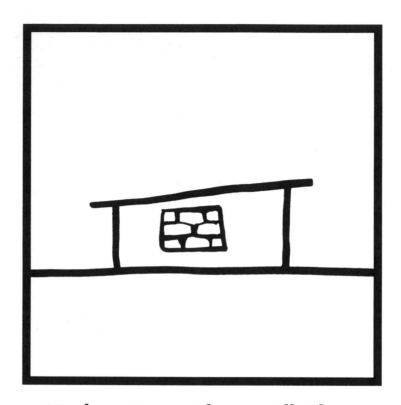

Modern Home That Is All Glass
Except the Windows Which Are Brick

This is actually more of a drawing than a Droodle but I've included it because I'm fond of Modern Architecture. You see, when I was young there was a period when we weren't too well off and we didn't have a big fancy house. We didn't have a little simple house either. We lived in a chicken coop. We didn't mind living in the chicken coop except in the morning when the farmer would come around and lift us up to look for eggs. This caused a draft and we younger children suffered constantly from colds. That's why I like houses with brick windows.

Piccolo Player As Seen from Inside Piccolo

If you don't understand this Droodle, what you see are the piccolo player's finger tips covering up the little holes in the piccolo. It's Droodles like this that cause troublemakers to write me letters saying I am "coo-koo." I do not appreciate these letters. I am not "coo-koo." These are the same type of Wrong Thinkers who always yell "shhushh" in movies when I'm explaining the important points of the plot to the girl whose way I paid in. Or who rap on the door of a telephone booth when I'm trying to catch a quick catnap. If you ask me, they are the ones who are "coo-koo" and they should be watched.

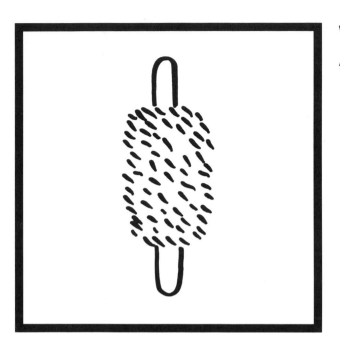

Worm Wearing an Angora Sweater

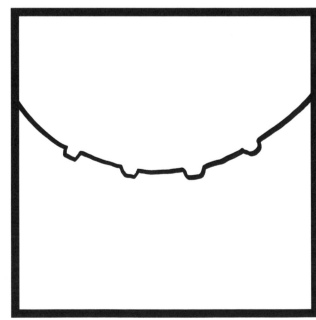

Cow on a Cold Morning

If you've never spent any time on a farm you probably won't understand this Droodle.

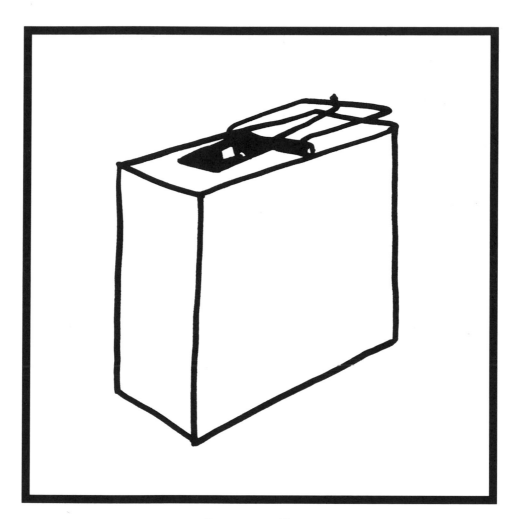

Trap for a Tall Mouse

Ostrich Hiding Head After Swallowing Telephone

Every time I look at this I get angry because the telephone pictured is mine. It is also my ostrich and he has hidden his head in my mattress and is probably right now eating another of my expensive inner springs (which were custom contour-shaped to keep me from sleeping round-shouldered). The phone has been ringing constantly and neither of us has been able to sleep all week. The ostrich's name is "Ick," a name I gave him because personal daintiness has remained a mystery to him (and he shows no interest in solving it). Frankly I'm afraid that Ick will have to go, which makes me unhappy because (a) he is basically an affectionate bird; (b) ostrich soup gives me indigestion.

Bubble Gum Champ

If you got this one, it shows you have a healthy attitude toward life and are fond of sports. However, if you prefer the alternate title:

Small Boy Throwing Baseball (at You)

you are apprehensive and nervous and should get a divorce and go live all alone in the mountains somewhere.

This Droodle was originally presented on my NBC television program in an anonymous state, and I offered $100 for the best title submitted (with $25 prizes for place and show). Over 30,000 Right Thinkers sent in answers, all of which were highly original. This prompted my partner, Leonard Stern, to observe, "The best thing about Droodles is that anyone can do them, and the worst thing about them is that everyone does." I'm not sure what he meant, but I assume it was complimentary.

The winning title was submitted by Miss Lois Kovell of Detroit. It was:

Rear View of Girl Wearing Earrings and Her Hair in a Bun Kissing Boy with Crew Cut

Among the other magnificent suggestions received was:

Father Stuffed Olive Protecting Babies from Attack by Porcupine

(Robert G. Carman, Cleveland Heights, Ohio)

These titles show what an excellent public service Droodles perform. How else could people get rid of ideas such as these, which normally would just lie around in their heads and get in the way when they were trying to add up the bill at the supermarket or cheat at canasta? A psychiatrist would charge a thousand dollars and take two and a half years to get rid of any one of these ideas. So don't take chances—if you've got any peculiar ideas about anything, start Droodling right away, before it's too late.

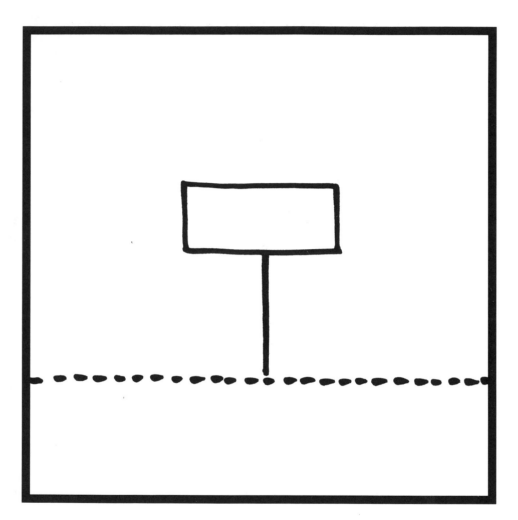

Sign on a Dotted Line

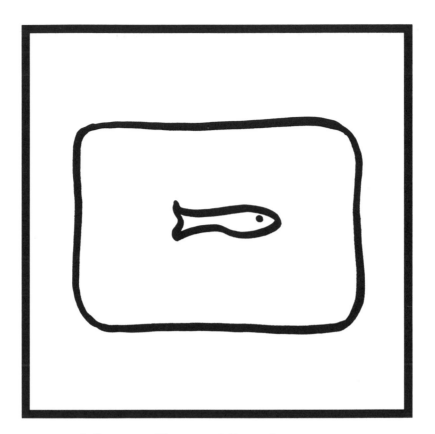

Rich Sardine with Private Can

This Droodle is one of the most thought provoking. If you are sensitive you will worry about it for at least twenty minutes because it poses certain questions: Why does this particular sardine have a private can? Did he strike oil in a codfish? Did he win a jackpot prize on a television program such as "Name that Tuna"? And if he is so rich why has he no friends? Couldn't he at least hire a valet to squeeze a lemon over him several times a day? He must be depressed and lonely. Frankly, I think this sardine should join a Friendship Club.

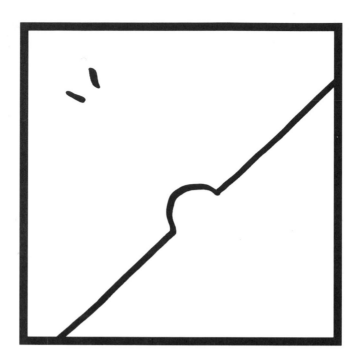

Mosquito Showing Girlfriend Latest Job

This Droodle should make you stop for a moment and consider the problems of the mosquito. They are conscientious, hard-working little insects. If a mosquito isn't rushing around collecting plasma, he's busy recording "buzz-buzz-buzzz-buzzes" for the telephone company to use when you dial a busy number. At night he has to work even harder humming around your bedroom keeping you awake. And half the time after he flies to the ceiling, executes a perfect wing-over and dives on you with all flaps up–you roll over and he winds up with a face full of mattress. Think how he feels. Frustrated, that's how. So next time you see a mosquito, remember his problems and encourage him by giving him a friendly slap on the back.

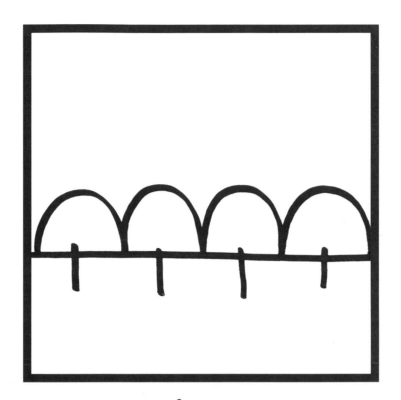

Start of a Rat Race

This Droodle is a favorite of mine because it has an alternate title which is possibly even more philosophical than the original. An alternate is:

Assembly Line in a Falsie Factory

Marc Connelly has suggested another title, but this one doesn't seem to make much sense:

Three Mushrooms and a Toadstool for Gourmets Who Like to Play Russian Roulette

Trellis with Suspenders to Hold Its Plants Up

You may find it hard to believe that there was once a time when there were no such things as suspenders. Suspenders were first invented in 308 B.C. (give or take a couple of months) by the Phoenicians who called them "slingshots." Several hundred years later the bow and arrow were introduced to the Phoenicians and in order to take care of the surplus slingshots, pants were invented. The original purpose of pants was to hold the suspenders down. However, they didn't because it was another 400 years before anyone invented buttons.

Even though they are no longer used as weapons, suspenders can still be dangerous. My brother Stanley who was a 97-pound weakling once bought a pair of powerful elastic suspenders. The elastic in the suspenders was so powerful that when Stanley wore them he couldn't walk. He hovered 6 inches above the floor. It didn't bother Stanley too much but it scared the bejabers out of the cat.

Navel Orange Wearing a Bikini Bathing Suit

This is a rather romantic Droodle and it makes some people think of far-off places such as the Riviera or Coney Island. It makes me think of my Uncle Parker. For a time back home, Uncle Parker was a garbage collector. He didn't work for the Sanitation Department—he just liked to collect garbage. He discovered this unusual hobby through plain "dumb luck" (something Uncle Parker had plenty of). One day when leaving home for work he accidentally picked up a package of garbage, mistaking it for his lunch. Uncle Parker didn't realize his mistake until he got home that night and Aunt Margaret told him what had happened. (He had been suspicious when he ate a grapefruit rind stuffed with coffee grounds at the noon hour, but he figured Aunt Margaret had been getting recipes from television again.) From that time on Uncle Parker began to collect garbage systematically, even though some of the townspeople—mainly the ones next door—made discouraging comments such as "Disgusting!" "Unsanitary!" and "Too revolutionary!" Eventually, he found a use for his garbage. He saw a sign in a store urging people to send CARE packages to our friends in Europe. So he took his garbage, made CARELESS packages and shipped them to Communists behind the Iron Curtain.

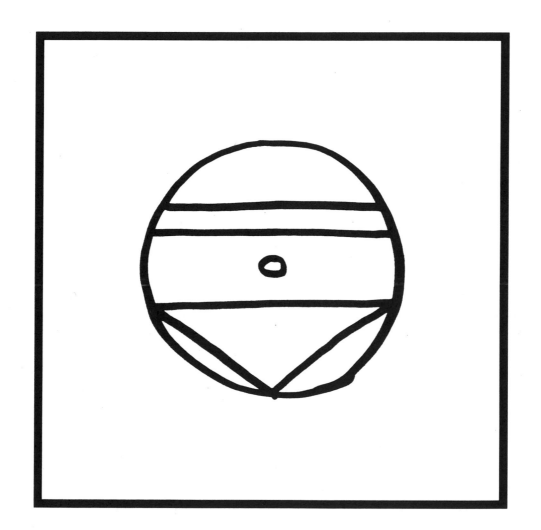

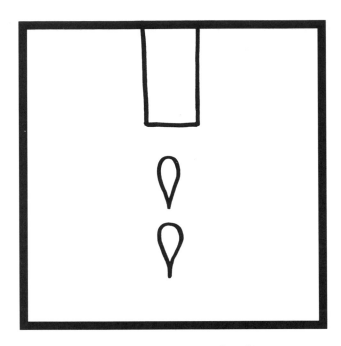

Water Faucet Inhaling

If you are at all sensitive you'll pause a moment and wonder why a water faucet should be inhaling. Did it hear there's a shortage and is it trying to conserve? Or is it actually sniffling sadly because the garbage disposal unit is choking on a chicken bone? Or perhaps it caught a cold from a drafty drainpipe? Life is filled with mysteries such as this.

The water faucet has an interesting history. It was invented by a man named Henry Clobb who was getting tired of having to stuff old newspapers, rags and his fingers into the ends of pipes to stop water from spurting all over his kitchen. If you don't believe this, run to your bathroom or kitchen and you'll see this man's initials right there on your faucet handles.

Butterfly Skipping Rope

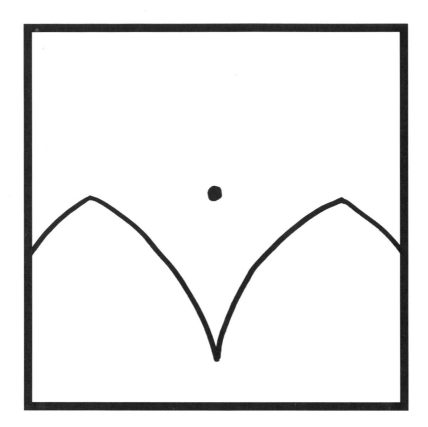

Ant on Shower-Room Floor
As Seen by Miss Patricia Del Ray

I have decided, out of deference to Miss Del Ray, to make no comment on this Droodle. Instead I will put down a few notes concerning ants.

On second thought, out of deference to the A.S.P.C.A., I won't say anything about ants. So I think I *will* say a few things about Miss Del Ray. *(Editor's note: Oh, no, you won't!)*

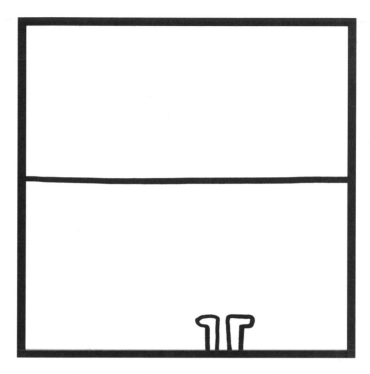

Clumsy Tightrope Walker

If you turn the Droodle upside down this could also be:

Small Girl with Large Balloon

Or again it might even be titled:

Lady Wearing the Ultimate in Uplift Bras

You may take your choice of any of these. If you got any of the correct answers, it shows you are honest, loyal, clean, trustworthy, wear a cute, little, expensive, brown uniform and help old ladies across the street.

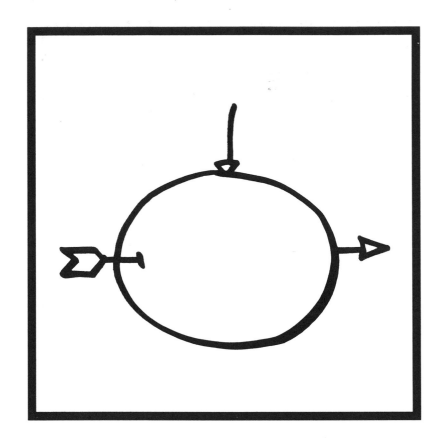

Brave Balloon

The balloon in this Droodle has been punctured clear through, but bravely refuses to collapse—which is more than I can say for a lot of people I know.

(It's statements such as the above which have given me a reputation as a deep thinker all over southern West Virginia. Also on West 58th Street in New York and in Van Nuys, California.)

Fish Fishing

A number of Troublemakers have claimed this Droodle is farfetched. "How come no bait on the hook?" they say. Or, "How could a fish tie a knot in a string?" Well, this fish isn't using bait because he's smart enough to realize that if he did he might catch himself. He's only interested in fishing—not catching. And if you look closely you'll see that the knot in the string was tied by the fish's grandmother as it is a granny knot. (I love to put in humorous lines like that last one so you can face the future with a smile. If you're not facing the future with a smile it shows you are too sophisticated. You should lead a simpler life and wear looser shoes.)

$25 Hamburger

If you don't think much of this Droodle, it shows you're having trouble living within your income and do not understand the beneficial aspects of our economic system, such as "inflation."

Thousands of years ago there was no such thing as money, men used what was called the "Barter System." In those days a man could get a good, slightly used wife for fifteen sheep. Today that same wife will cost him at least fifty sheep. This is what is known as inflation.

Note: Mr. Rice just read this page and he claims that the illustration I gave is fallacious. In fact he has offered me his wife for only four sheep and has agreed to throw in his new seersucker sports coat and a jar of pickled onions. But I am sure he was just being facetious. After all, what would he do with four sheep in New York City? He wouldn't even have a place to keep them. When I pointed this out to him and complimented him on his sly sense of humor he agreed with me and went back to the kitchen and began singing "Melancholy Baby" again. You know a song like that can eventually get on a person's nerves. I must speak to the publishers about a higher royalty rate.

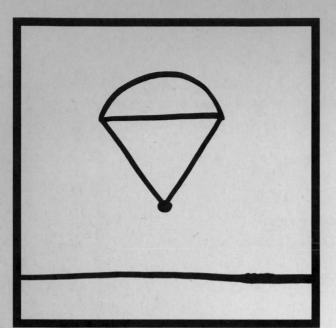

**Cowardly Fly
Making a Landing**

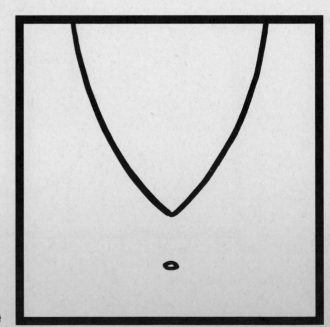

Rocket Ship Landing on a Dime

98

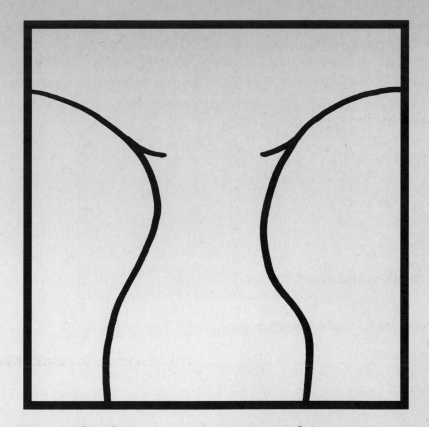

Two Elephants Not on Speaking Terms

If you keep staring at this Droodle long enough one of two things will happen: (1) You will develop eyestrain and go to bed; (2) You will see that it might also be a picture of a lady with her arms extended which could be titled:

TV Model Preparing to Demonstrate Deodorant

Full Moon Seen at Sing Sing

Prison reform is the subject of a lot of discussion these days, especially among prisoners. I have some knowledge of the situation that exists in prisons because my no-good brother Duke was once given a "vacation by the government" as we refer to it back home and Duke didn't adjust too well. One day while he was working on the rock pile making little ones out of big ones under a broiling hot sun, Duke's resentment boiled up inside him and he raised his 40-lb. sledgehammer and brought it down on the warden's skull.

There was a rule against this.

So, they took away Duke's commissary charge account for 6 weeks. It made Duke so mad he refused to participate in the next 3 riots. This shows how lack of understanding can make a man anti-social.

Twenty Below Zero

ZZZZZZZ

**Laundromat for
Basketball Players**

Two Comic-Strip Characters in a Manhole with Nothing to Say to Each Other

When I flunked out of Art School for the second time, I decided to get even with them by becoming a great comic-strip artist. I also decided to make myself the hero of the strip because I had more interesting things to say than anyone else I knew. But I ran into trouble right away. In the first strip that I prepared, my talk-balloon crowded out all of the characters including me. So in the next strip I introduced a teensy-weensy character named Oscar, who could fit in the corner of the strip and who said things like "What?" and "You can say that again!" and I would say it again.

It was a fascinating strip but, unfortunately, newspaper editors were too hide bound and unimaginative to appreciate it, so I got even with the art school another way. I grew a beard and enrolled again under an assumed name.

Depressed Flea Committing Suicide

Unlike the Rich Sardine, this flea is not depressed because he is lonely. He suffers from copelessness (inability to cope*) just as most people do and for the same reasons.

You probably never realized it but fleas are constantly faced with decisions. First, they must decide whether to hang out on a high-class dog or a low-class human. If they pick a dog they must then decide whether to take a short-haired terrier so they can get a suntan or a silky, long-haired collie so their friends will say, "My, what a nice place you have here," when they come to visit.

If the flea picks a human, he will gain something in prestige but he will be in constant danger. Humans don't scratch as well as dogs do (especially with their hind legs), but they have other more serious disadvantages. For one thing they take a lot of unnecessary baths and the flea could drown. Humans also get hit by automobiles, stick their fingers in wet paint and get haircuts. All of this means danger to the flea. Believe me, a flea leads a dog's life.

*In One Head and Out the Other, Chapter IV.

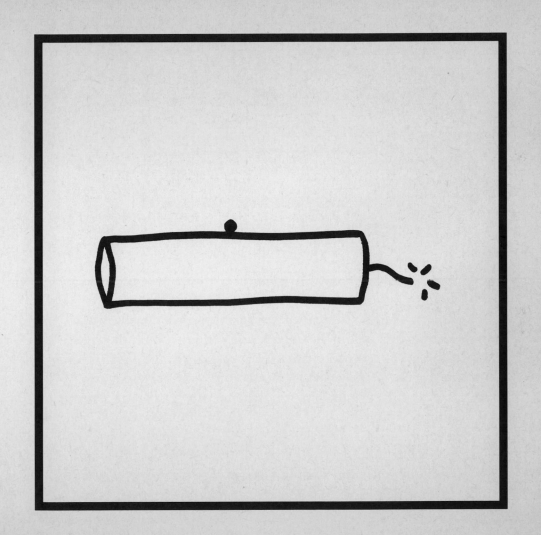

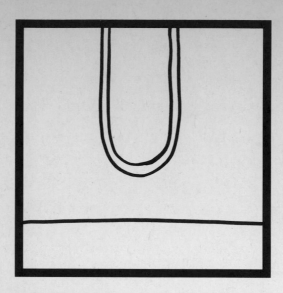

Fire Pole for False Alarms

This Droodle reminds me of an idea I once had for a fire truck for false alarms (it had no wheels). It also reminds me of Ed Simms. Back home in Sissonsville, Ed Simms was the most popular man in town with us children. We all thought he was a real storybook hero. You see, Ed was the entire fire department in Sissonsville and took his job very seriously. He was always studying correspondence courses in fire-fighting techniques such as: "Door Smashing," "Cat Rescuing" and "Checker Playing." Unfortunately (for Ed) we never had any fires in Sissonsville, but he was too conscientious to let that stop him. Regular as clockwork, every Monday morning Ed would bust into someone's house, chop up a couple of pieces of furniture with his axe, squirt water on all the men, and carry all the women outside with a fireman's lift.

Ed wasn't so popular with the grown-ups.

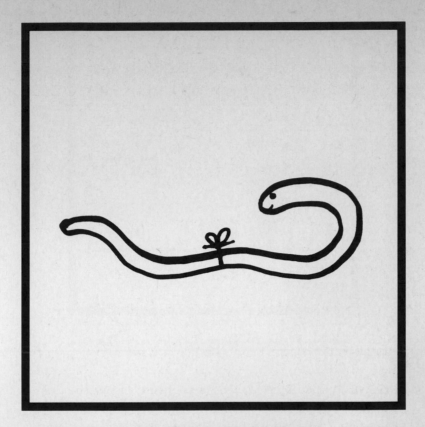

Absent-Minded Worm

An extremely well-drawn Droodle, showing a fine sense of design, proportion and anatomy. You will notice that the bowknot is also accurately drawn. A highly technical Droodle such as this is not for the amateur (you).

Ship Deserting Sinking Rats

This Droodle, thought up by Judith Broker (age 10) of Los Angeles, is unusually brilliant. I've always thought the expression, "Rats deserting a sinking ship" was ridiculous. What else should they do? Stay on board and drown like rats?

Many people are unfair to rats and shudder when they hear the word. Actually rats make delightful pets and can be taught amusing tricks. With patience you can teach a rat to gnaw furniture, steal food or scare the daylights out of your grandmaw. And when training these friendly little creatures you need take only the simplest of precautions. Wear heavy leather gloves, carry a baseball bat, keep your throat covered and memorize the phone number of a doctor who can administer anti-rabies shots.

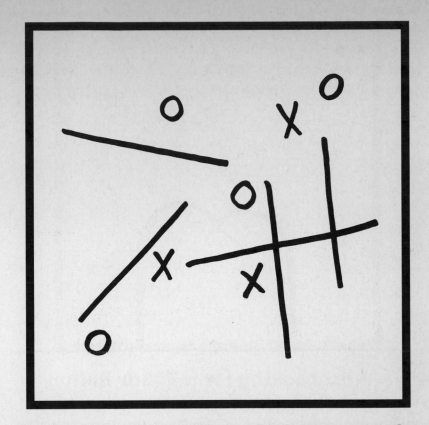

Tic-Tac-Toe Game Played by Two Drunks

It seems to me that this Droodle pretty well explains itself, but I suppose some readers will say they have not got their money's worth unless I put something down here. This grasping, greedy sort of reader is not the sort we want for this book *(Publisher's Note: Mr. Price is wrong)*, and I am not going to be intimidated into saying another word about the Droodle.

Nudist Looking for a Collar Button

Not many of the people I've tested with this Droodle get it right. I must admit that it is a difficult one because it poses a question—"What would a nudist want with a collar button?"

However, there is an answer to this question. The answer is: "None of your business."

As you can see, these Droodles make a lot more sense than you might think at first glance.

The alternate title for this Droodle is:

Croquet Wicket for Siamese Twins

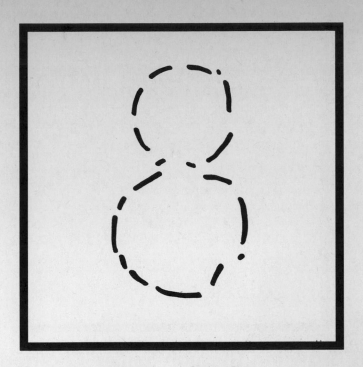

Pieces of Eight

Pieces of eight is a name given to an ancient Spanish silver coin which was worth eight reales. This coin was also called a *peso* by the Spaniards and *loot* by the English, many of whom were pirates at the time. In those days, pirates sailed under a flag that looked like an iodine label and sank ships and captured pretty women and stabbed each other and drank grog and stayed up all night and shot off cannons. Believe me, fellows like that would have a hard time keeping an apartment in New York today.

The only pirates around nowadays are the ones in Pittsburgh who are very good-natured and never cause anyone any trouble, except the Giants occasionally.

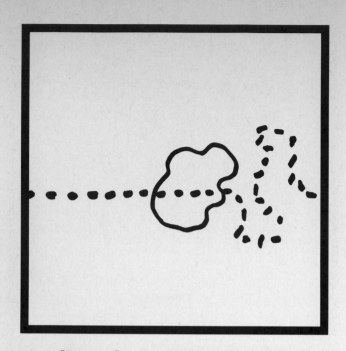

Ants Crawling Through Spilled Champagne

Ants! Scientists have been hollering for years about what hard workers ants are. I say, "Ha!" If you ask me, they're nothing but no-good, worthless little bums. If they're so industrious and such hard workers, how come they have to go around stealing food all the time And another thing—if they're so conscientious about always keeping on the job, why do they spend so much time at picnics?

Personally, I'll take the grasshopper as a symbol of industry any day. Grasshoppers are a prettier color than ants, have much better posture, and are always engaged in some *commendable, worthwhile* activity such as high jumping, spitting tobacco juice or appearing in Walt Disney Pictures. You never catch a grasshopper swiping sugar.

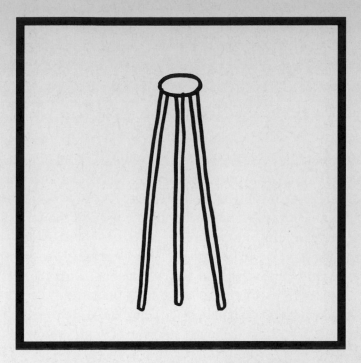

Stool for Milking Giraffes

This Droodle was given to me by Percy Barker whose company, Monogram of California, puts out Droodle cocktail napkins which everyone says are more fun than a pocketful of yogurt, or having a tooth pulled without novocaine. In order to boost sales I recently suggested to Percy that he give away a leaky glass with every box of napkins but he was too shortsighted to see the commercial value of this idea. Percy also turned down the opportunity to market several other interesting inventions developed by the Schwine-Kitzenger Institute and myself. For instance, a water pistol that shoots sand for kids who live in Death Valley. Or an even more useful item: an overarm deodorant for people who are ticklish.

Tall Cow

This Droodle, of course, is absurdly obvious. You will notice that the cow portrayed is the old-fashioned model without the extra faucet for yogurt. Cows are friendly beasts who supply us with milk and are frequently used to motivate the plot in Western movies. The cow has been variously described as: (1) *bovinus domesticus* (Webster); (2) a large animal that carries around a bowling ball with the holes inside out (Bob Hope); (3) an animal that, from the front, looks like a catcher signaling for a curve (Al Schwartz); (4) a creature who carries about a skin valise (Gary Moore).

Cows are gentle creatures and such antisocial activities as murder, hijacking, arson* and robbery are unknown among them. And unlike certain bipeds, whom I will not embarrass by mentioning here, no cow has ever been known to say any thing sillier than, "Mooo."

The cow is also sensitive and if you should happen to run across one, try to say something flattering to it.

*With one exception—a cow belonging to a Mrs. O'Leary of Chicago, IL.

Accordion That Has Just Been Cleaned and Pressed

This Droodle requires no comment from me (or from you either), which gives me an opportunity to set something straight. Too many people (several to be exact) have been confusing Droodles with noodles. There's no connection. Noodles are little strips of dried dough sometimes served with cheese and tomato sauce. While Droodles may be etched into flat slices of cheese and served with tomato sauce, they are not strips of dough. However, in all fairness, I must admit that when I boiled a few Droodles with a beef bone and some carrots they were rather tasty (had a superb beef bone and carrot flavor).

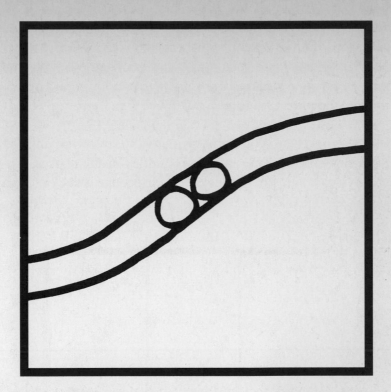

Two Corpuscles Who Loved in Vein

Certain Wrong Thinkers may say this Droodle, sent to me by Marian Verilli of Scarsdale, New York, is silly. Not so! In fact, it has inspired me to write a story about two newlywed corpuscles named Ruthie Red and Willie White who saved up enough penicillin to buy a home right off a main artery, centrally located near the solar plexus. They had a wonderful honeymoon visiting Ruthie's relatives down south in the toes and Willie's family out west in the fingers. On the way back they stopped off at the stomach and watched a glass of water cascading down the esophagus, and spent the night in the lungs for some fresh air. Come to think of it, maybe this Droodle is silly.

Now I think it's time that I make the supreme sacrifice and reveal to you the secret of how to make your own Droodles. Noted educators and sociologists have begged me not to do this, but I'm determined. Droodling is not for a limited, intellectual elite. It is for everybody.

First, to make sure you're ready, study the following untitled Droodles and write in your correct titles in the spaces provided for same. Then check the correct answers on page 121.

1. _____

2. _____

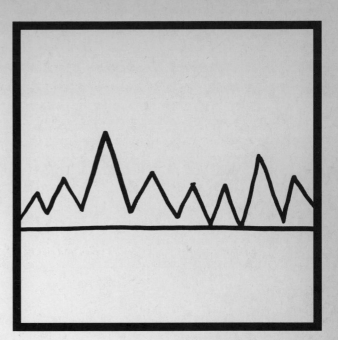

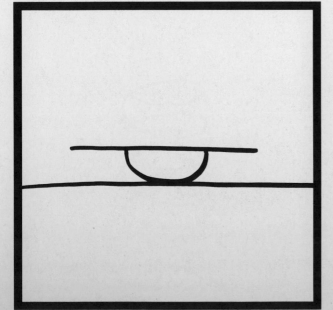

3. _____

4. _____

5. _____

1. Stork Wearing Argyle Socks

2. Manhattan Skyline in 1492

3. Fried Egg, Sunny Side Down

4. Worm Walking on Tiptoe

5. Two Bugs Making Love in the Spring

If you got any of the titles correct give yourself 20 points. If you understand any of the titles after seeing the correct answer give yourself 10 points. If you think any of them make sense give yourself 5 points.

If your total score is 2 or over, you are ready to start making your own Droodles.

So, set your affairs in order, pack a clean shirt, say good-bye to your family, take a deep breath and turn the page.

Here is my secret method of making Droodles. Below you will find the 14 basic shapes, and a number of psychologically tested forms that can be cut out and pushed around until they form a pattern or design that looks like a Droodle.

Here are the basic shapes:

Got the shapes all cut out and pushed around until they form a Droodle? Good. Now all that's left for you to do is give it a title. You can approach the problem in exactly the same way. Following are all the letters you will need to write a brilliant and witty title. Cut them out and push them around until they form one.

A   B   C   D   E

F   G   H   I   J

K   L   M   N   O

P   Q   R   S   T

U   V   W   X   Y

            Z

Droodles stimulate the imagination. What does this Droodle
look like to you? It might be

A Grapefruit with a Sight for Aiming Squirts

or it might be

A Hairbrush with No Bristles for Bald-Headed Men

It also might be

A Cowardly Tennis Racket with No Guts

It might even be

Lump with a Hook
So It Can Be Hung in the Lump Closet

But it isn't. The correct title for this Droodle is:

A Sassy Olive Sticking Out Its Pimiento

Now you have the idea. I have, anyway. So you can plunge
into all of Droodles with the knowledge that you are going to
emerge a wiser, more stimulated person. Especially if you
read the commentary I have included at no extra expense to
you. I have spent much valuable time writing this commentary and making it philosophical, witty and thought provoking. Study it carefully. Read between the lines.

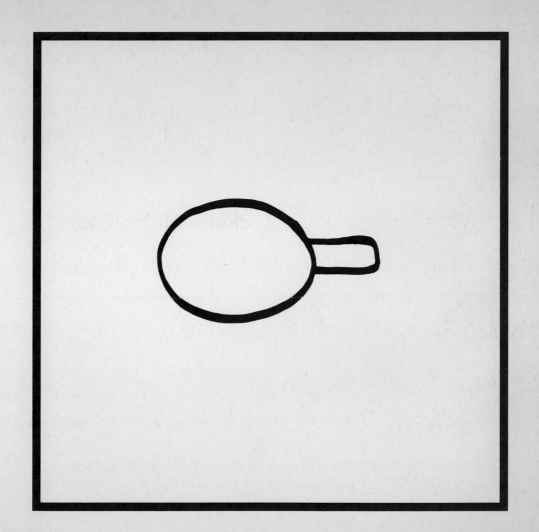

Roger Price, one of the founders of Price Stern Sloan, was a well-known artist, comedian and writer appearing on TV and radio for over two decades.

Early in his career, he was a gag writer for Bob Hope, and Kenny Delmar's variety show, "School House." He was half of Lud and Luster on "The Jimmy Dean Show," and a regular on "Name's the Same," "What Happened" and "Who's There."

In the 1950s, Price's Droodles became the basis for an outrageous TV quiz show that challenged celebrity panelists and home viewers to guess the names of these odd line drawings.

Price's other books include the best-selling party game *Madlibs,* which he co-created with partner Leonard Stern, *In One Head and Out the Other, J.G. the Upright Ape, The Roob Revolution* and *Me First.*